Proving God With Numbers

SECOND EDITION

STEVEN C. MOXHAM

ISBN:

ISBN-13: 978-0-473-47378-5 (Paperback)
ISBN-13: 978-0-473-47379-2 (Epub)
ISBN-13: 978-0-473-47380-8 (Kindle)

Originally published on March 23, 2019, New Zealand.

COVER IMAGES

Front Cover:

"Numbers from Heaven". Concept by Steven C. Moxham. Designed by Cherie Fox Design.

Back Cover Photos:

1. Looking over the Temple Mount complex in Jerusalem. Credit: Steven C. Moxham
2. The author being 'kissed' by a camel in Bethany on the Mt. of Olives in the West Bank (al-Eizariya) Credit: Camel owner.

CONTENTS

New In This Edition   i

Prologue   iii

Introduction   v

1   Talking with God   1

2   Divine Inspiration   8

3   Forgiveness & Letting Go   17

4   Israel & The Number 7   20

5   7 Months   25

6   7 Years   32

7   70 Years   35

8   Closing Arguments   46

9   12 Weeks   51

10 Donald Trump & The Number 7   60

11 Messages From God: Life After Death   68

    - First Message   74

    - Second Message   77

    - Third Message   80

    Further Reading   82

NEW IN THIS EDITION

- New chapter 9: "12 Weeks"
- Updated chapter 10: "Donald Trump & The Number 7"

PROLOGUE

On August 29, 2018, while lying in bed at night trying to go to sleep, God put it in my heart to write this book. I initially tried to ignore it and brush it off as a random thought, however, the Spirit seemed insistent, and so I got up later that night and started to write this book. Therefore, I know that it was God's will that I wrote this book. If therefore you are reading this book, then there is probably a good reason that you are doing so! Perhaps there is something in this book that God wants you to see, or read.

If that is the case, then I hope that you will be blessed by what you are about to read.

God Bless.

Steve Moxham
September 20, 2018

INTRODUCTION

As the title suggests, this book is about using numbers to prove that God exists.

I am not a theologian, nor a biblical scholar, nor even a member of a church! I am simply a layman who, through time and experience, has come to see the very real divine hand of God at work in my life.

I hope to use those experiences to prove to you that God exists, and is a very real ever-present force in our lives.

"Man's goings are of the Lord; How can a man then understand his own way?" – Proverbs 20:24.

1. TALKING WITH GOD

Since I am trying to prove to you that there is a divine spiritual presence out there that governs our everyday lives, I am going to start with probably the most significant spiritual interaction that I have had with that presence that we call God.

It came about as a result of something that happened over a year earlier, that had a significantly negative impact on my life. Back in late 2009, I was in the process of selling my website business GoForex.net to an internet-based company in the United States. Essentially, I wanted more for the business than they offered me, and so the deal ultimately collapsed. Unfortunately for me, I knew that these were the people that I was meant to sell my website to, but not for the price that they offered me!

As a result of not selling my website to this business, my life went slowly backwards over the next eight and a half years. This was no surprise to me, because I knew that what should have happened didn't, and so it led to me not being in the right place at the right time to take up the opportunities that were presented to me.

No doubt that will be a familiar story to some of you reading this, just in a different way! Such are the trials and tribulations of life. Life is a tapestry of highs and lows, successes and failures, joys and disappointments, triumphs and tragedies! That is the lot we have been given.

So after just over a year since that big disappointment that had a life-changing impact on my life, I had what I would still describe as the most significant experience or interaction with God that I have ever had!

While I was lying in bed, either late at night or very early in the morning – I can't remember which now – I suddenly felt the divine presence of God come upon me, and I immediately knew what He wanted me to do! God wanted me to ask Him how much my website was worth to the company that approached me to buy it over a year earlier. So I did.

It was an amazing feeling to know that I was in the presence of God, and that He had come to me to get me to ask Him a question!

So I started to pray. This is what I said: "How much was my website worth to (said company)?" And then I started at a certain figure. "$550,000?" All this was done through the spirit, not out loud. Instead of replying, I felt God pulling me higher. "$650,000?" Nope. Higher still. "$750,000?" I kept doing this, until I felt the Spirit of God stop me at US$1250K ($1.25 million). It was like hitting a brick wall! There was absolutely no doubt that this was the figure that God was telling me that my website was worth to the company that approached me to buy it.

Once I was satisfied that this was the correct figure that God wanted me to know, I ended my prayer, and His Spirit left me. I remember lying in bed afterwards thinking, 'Wow, that was amazing!', and 'why didn't I think of doing that before?' Of course, it wasn't me that prompted it, God came to me because He wanted me to know something, maybe for my own benefit, but perhaps for everyone else's as well.

So there I had it. God told me that my website was worth US$1.25 million to the company that wanted to buy it, and who I wanted to sell it to, but their offer paled in comparison! So what was God trying to tell me here? That I was right to reject their offer, even though it had a terrible impact on my life by not accepting it? I guess that was part of it, but there may have been a greater purpose for doing so further down the track.

I was somewhat perplexed by that number, US$1.25 million. It didn't mean anything to me, other than the fact it was $250,000 above my initial asking price when I first put up my website for sale back in August 2009. And that's the way it remained for several months.

Then, for some unknown reason, I went back and looked at the valuation document that I had sent the proposed buyer. What I discovered astounded me.

There, in black and white, I had calculated that my website would have added approximately US$2.5 million to the buyer's market value on the Nasdaq Stock Exchange at the time. And that's when I realised the significance of what God had told me my website was worth to this company.

US$1.25 million is exactly half the US$2.5 million that I had calculated that my website would add to their market capitalisation. The company was worth approximately US$350 million on the Nasdaq Stock Exchange at the time, and so it was a simple matter for me to calculate exactly how much my website would add to their market value.

They were trading at around 32 times after-tax profit, otherwise known as the Price/Earnings (P/E) ratio, and so all I had to do was take my pre-tax profit, use their effective tax rate, and multiply it by their P/E ratio. That figure came to approximately US$2.5 million. I had completely forgotten about that number from a year earlier, when I had created the valuation document, and the only number that I had remembered was US$3.4 million as the projected worth of my website to this company, one year after buying it.

So to discover this number was absolutely amazing to me!

What God was essentially telling me was that my website was worth US$1.25 million to them, because they would have doubled their money upon its acquisition! They would have bought my website at a discount to its actual economic value to them, and thereby doubled their money! So that is why God told me what my website was worth to them. It validated my own valuation of US$1 million, and confirmed to me that I wasn't asking anything above what God thought it was valued at.

I would have accepted less for my website; however, I wasn't even offered anything close to my asking price! I had received previous offers from other companies, but either the terms of the deal weren't right, or the company wasn't right. When this Nasdaq-listed company came along, I knew that these were the people that I was meant to sell my business to, but their offer was so far below my expectations, that I couldn't sell it to them! It was actually lower than previous offers I had received from other people and rejected!

So unfortunately, the deal collapsed. And that meant that at this 'fork in the road', my life would take a backwards direction, instead of a forwards one!

Could I have accepted 50% of something rather than 100% of nothing? Yes, absolutely. However, it should be a reasonable expectation to expect that a buyer offers a fair and reasonable price, in order to feel that both parties are getting something out of the deal. If it only feels one-way, then one party will be happy, while the other one goes away unhappy. To me, that is not the right way to do business. Everyone should feel like they have come away with something. To me, this was an "our way, or the highway" type of deal! And that is not the right way to do business, even if they think they are doing the right thing for their shareholders. Ultimately everyone comes away with nothing, and no one wins! It's a lose-lose for all.

Still, that wasn't the only thing that God would do to verify that my conversation with Him was real.

About two years later in January 2013, I was going through my old emails, when I discovered the last email that I received from the company that had approached me to buy it in November 2009. While I was looking at this final email in the acquisition process, I discovered something quite amazing!

The last email that I received from this company arrived at exactly 12:50PM on December 24, 2009 – Christmas Eve. I couldn't believe it! That was the exact number that God had stopped me on in my conversation with Him! $1250K or US$1.25 million. So here I had the very last email in the acquisition process, arriving at the exact number that God had told me my website was worth to them, over a year after receiving their final offer.

You see, when I got to $1,050,000 in my questioning with God, I didn't say "one million and fifty thousand", I said "ten-fifty(K)", and so on, until He stopped me at US$1250K, or "twelve-fifty(K)", meaning US$1.25 million. So the number that He stopped me on of US$1250K, was exactly the same as you would read it on the clock as 12:50PM.

So on top of the calculation in my valuation document, together with this last email arriving at 12:50PM, God had essentially verified my conversation with Him that my website was worth US$1.25 million to them.

So now I had two real-life confirmations to support my claim of having had a conversation with God. I knew it was real – I didn't need any confirmations to tell me as much, but in terms of backing up my claims, this was incredible!

2. DIVINE INSPIRATION

About two and a half weeks before my direct conversation with God, I had what I consider to be another supernatural experience from Him. On December 26, 2010 (Boxing Day), while I was sitting outside on a rock enjoying the early afternoon sun, in a somewhat heightened sense of expectation; I suddenly felt something come down from above my head, and down into my body. As it did, I instantaneously knew everything about a new business idea in a moment of time.

It had been almost one year to the day since I had received the last email from the company that was supposed to have bought my last business on December 24, 2009, and this appeared to be the next business that God wanted me to set up. I still owned GoForex.net, but it should have been sold a year ago.

The concept for this business was one I was familiar with. It would be a proprietary share trading business that invested money with various traders to trade the share market on my behalf. I would start with $250,000, divided up over five initial traders, who would form the foundation of my new business. These traders would then trade the New Zealand stock market on my behalf, and we would divide up the profits at a predetermined rate.

Unlike a traditional proprietary trading firm that employs traders, trains them up and situates them in their own building, my business would instead seek out already successful share traders who trade from home, and allow them to use their own proprietary share trading strategies. I would simply be leveraging their expertise using my own capital. Today, this is known as the "gig economy".

In addition to being given the concept for this business, I was also given various details about it, including where I would take the business, and how I would sell it.

Interestingly, Hong Kong was the only place that God gave me as a secondary place to take the business to, besides New Zealand. Although New Zealand was not specifically mentioned – it didn't need to be – because I was always going to set it up there first before taking it overseas, and then branch out to other countries. It is a business model that is eminently suited to transferring to other countries.

In addition to setting up in Hong Kong, I also had plans to take it to the United States, the U.K. and Canada, in addition to New Zealand. To that end, I registered trademarks in all five of these countries in early 2011.

Only two-to-three years earlier in 2007/08, the world suffered what is commonly referred to as the "Global Financial Crisis" or GFC for short. Stock markets tumbled, currencies plummeted, and property markets fell. It was extremely easy to make money on plummeting currencies, so much so that even I jumped in and made some easy thousands! You didn't even have to think. Just sell! That was one upside to the financial volatility that hit the markets over that time.

A few years on, in late 2010 when I was given this idea to set up a business trading shares on the share market, it was still far from certain which way economies were going to go, and there was a lot of fear and speculation in the media about the fragility of global markets and which direction they were heading in. I had no such concern! I had been given a divinely inspired business idea, and I KNEW that it *would* succeed! I had absolutely no doubt whatsoever.

Effectively, that meant that global economies had to recover in order for my business to do well, because it relied on stocks and shares going up in order for my business to succeed. So that is the conclusion that I came to. Markets must be going to go up, or otherwise my business wouldn't succeed; or at least, it wouldn't be as successful as it could be. And that is indeed what has happened.

On August 22, 2018, U.S. stock markets were

reported to have reached their longest bull run in history, beginning from a low on March 9, 2009. Other markets from around the world, including New Zealand, have had similar-length bull runs. In fact, if you look at a chart of the New Zealand share market index called the NZX 50, you will see that it also reached a low in March of 2009. After a relatively good 2009, our market went sideways for a couple of years until 2012, when it started a brilliant linear curve upwards for nearly seven years, as of August 2018.

What that meant for me is that God's timing was absolutely perfect, assuming I was able to launch this new business!

I was intending to launch this business around mid-2011, about six months after receiving the idea from God. I had paid for a legal opinion, registered trademarks and websites, changed my company name, and written a more extensive business plan going forward. The only thing that I was lacking was the capital, and that was meant to come from selling my old business to the Nasdaq-listed company that approached me to buy it.

As that didn't happen, I was unable to launch this new business!

I considered other methods of funding the business, including getting in outside shareholders, crowd funding, or even getting a bank loan, however, none of these methods either appealed or came to fruition, and so I was left to watch this opportunity go up in smoke!

If you look at a chart of the NZX 50 Index, you can see exactly how perfect God's timing was, had I been able to sell my old business and set up this new one.

Assuming that I had launched it in mid-2011 as my intention was, there was a slight dip in the market until about the start of 2012, before the market began its long rise up to record-breaking levels. From the time that this business was intended to have been launched in mid-2011 to the beginning of 2012, that time would have been taken up in finding and acquiring my traders to trade the share market on my behalf. So by the time 2012 rolled around, I would have been all set to go with my traders' trading the New Zealand share market, and dividing up the profits.

In the following chart you can see exactly what I am talking about.

10-Year Performance of the NZX 50 Index to September 28, 2018.

Source: Yahoo! Finance

Some years later, it suddenly struck me that I had probably missed out on about $30-$40 million in lost wealth, as a result of not being able to set up this new business! However, it is not just me who has missed out. I was intending to donate 10% of my traders' gross profits to various charities, so the wealth that could have been generated over the last seven years wasn't able to be shared with those less fortunate than myself.

What surprises me is that you can actually lose some of the things that God had intended for you to have, as a result of Him allowing free will to interfere with His plans.

I often think back to the story of Moses in the book of Numbers 20:8-12, where God required him to speak to a rock, and the water would flow out of it. Instead of doing so, he struck the rock twice, against God's instructions. As a result of that, he was not allowed to enter into the promised land of Israel, and died before ever setting foot on it.

God's original intention had been for Moses to enter into Israel, but because God had given Moses free will to make up his own mind, God allowed His own plans for Moses to be discarded, as a result of his own disobedience.

So it is clear to me that just because God intends for something to happen a certain way, doesn't mean that He is going to force it to be that way. Sometimes He allows for free will to interfere with His plans.

This is what I believe happened to me.

Something went wrong in the acquisition process of my previous business, meaning that I wasn't able to take up God's original plans and set up this new business. Nothing is set in stone unless God says it is! We can lose parts of God's plan for our life, if He allows it. That doesn't mean that God didn't know it was going to happen, it just means that sometimes He allows the consequences of our own, or others' actions to override His own desires for our lives. But hopefully He has a back-up plan in place!

ONE OTHER INTERESTING ASPECT to this divinely inspired business idea, was how I would sell it.

When I received this idea, there were two options for selling the business, however, one was hidden from my eyes. I am unsure why, but it didn't seem to matter which option I took for selling the business. The first option was to list it on the New Zealand Stock Exchange as a listed company. The name of the business was going to be called "Mantis Capital Investments, Ltd", after the Praying Mantis.

Whatever the second option was for selling the business, I wasn't allowed to see, so I will never know exactly what that was, unless God decides to reveal it to me at a later time.

How long this global market bull-run will go on for is anybody's guess. I wasn't given any time frames or dates for how long I would own this business for before selling it, so I can't give you any insight into how long this bull market will keep running for before it comes to an end!

What I do know is that God knows the future before we do, and can align us to take advantage of that if we allow Him to!

3. FORGIVENESS & LETTING GO

In early April 2012, while I was sitting watching the TV, I suddenly received the strongest inspiration to do something that I have ever received.

It was very clear, unlike anything else that I have ever received before or since.

That message was to read Revelation chapter 22. My immediate thoughts were, "is there even a Revelation chapter 22?" So I got up, went to my room and picked up my Bible. Sure enough, there it was! Revelation chapter 22. The last chapter of the book of Revelation, and the last chapter of the entire Bible.

I wasn't sure what I was supposed to see, so I started to read the chapter.

About half way through reading Revelation

chapter 22, I suddenly found what God had wanted me to see:

"He that is unjust, let him be unjust still: and he which is filthy, let him be filthy still: and he that is righteous, let him be righteous still: and he that is holy, let him be holy still. And, behold, I come quickly; and my reward is with me, to give every man according as his work shall be." – Revelation 22:11-12

I knew exactly what this referred to! It literally jumped out at me, and left a big impression on me.

What God was wanting to tell me was not to worry if people treat you badly or wrongly, because eventually He will repay everyone for their deeds, whether good or bad.

The fact that God had to tell me what my old website was worth to the people who were supposed to buy it, and that their offer was so far below what either I or God had valued it at; and that by not accepting their offer it had a devastating impact on my life, God was essentially telling me not to worry about those who are "unjust". He will eventually repay everyone for their deeds!

I think God has a certain expectation upon everyone to behave in a certain way, and if we fail to live up to that expectation, we can expect to see consequences in our lives!

I believe that this was God's way of helping me to deal with a big disappointment in my life, and to allow me to 'forgive' and let go of something that had a big impact on my life!

I was initially reluctant to add this experience to my testimony, because I didn't have any way of backing up my claim that this message to read Revelation chapter 22 came from God. However, on reflection, the verses that I found within the chapter were in fact a kind of 'proof' that this message came from God, because of the impact that they had on me, and the way that they 'spoke' to me in such a profound way.

So I am happy to include it here if it makes a difference for anybody else reading this message!

4. ISRAEL & THE NUMBER 7

Anyone who has a cursory knowledge of the Bible, will recognise the importance of the number seven to the Holy scriptures.

Right from Genesis 2:2 through to the book of Revelation, the number seven has an important place in the Bible. But it's not just the number seven that is important, it is also multiples of the number seven such as 70 and 49 (7 x 7).

The number seven has been woven into the tapestry and history of the Bible and Israel over more than a thousand years. One of the most important prophecies in the Bible relates to the coming of Jesus Christ as the Messiah of Israel. This prophecy in Daniel 9:24-27 allocates "70 weeks" to the people of Israel to usher in the Messiah, from the decree to rebuild Jerusalem after the 70-year period of exile in Babylon. This "70 weeks" is commonly accepted to mean 70 x 7 = 490 years.

So right throughout the Bible the number seven has a special place and meaning to God. Many interpret it as a number of "completeness" or "perfection".

So you can imagine my surprise when God started giving me trips to Israel and marking them with the number seven! To me it did two things; 1. It backed up the veracity of the Bible with its frequent use of the number seven; and 2. It was a way of confirming for me that God was indeed the inspiration behind my trips to Israel.

I had always wanted to visit Israel from the time I became a Christian, but it never really crossed my mind to actually go. That was until April 2010.

While I was sitting on the settee in my motel room, not thinking about anything, nonchalantly staring into the kitchen; all of a sudden, the idea came out of nowhere to visit Israel for the first time. Over time, I have come to realise that this is how God tends to communicate with me in most cases. He will give me some information or inspiration, coupled with spirit or power, that moves me to act. This was one of those occasions!

It was if a light bulb had gone off in my head. Within several minutes of receiving the idea to go to Israel, I was headed out the door and down to the local bookshop to buy a travel guide to Israel.

Later that night I sent an email to my dad, letting him know that I was thinking of visiting Israel for the first time. I didn't know it at the time, but this would later come in handy for verifying the actual date that this idea was given to me.

Exactly four weeks later on the 8th of May, I purchased economy class tickets to Israel, leaving on the 29th of May 2010, and returning on the 17th of June.

Having not sold my website four months earlier, I decided the prudent thing to do would be to buy economy class tickets, rather than upgrade to business class as I had done three months earlier on a trip to Singapore. The purpose of that trip was to view a mock-up of a new Embraer Phenom 300 jet at the Singapore Air Show in February 2010. I had plans to set up a private jet charter business based in Queenstown, New Zealand at the time, although these plans came to nothing after failing to sell my website a month earlier.

However, only six days out from departure, I decided that I would upgrade to business class instead. The very next day on the 24th of May, I paid the $13,500 for a return business class ticket to Israel.

At about the same time, I started monitoring a new client account in my forex affiliate back-office. From the 24th of May – the day I purchased these business class tickets – this one trader earned me approximately $7,000 over the next seven trading days, $12,000 in two weeks, and more than $15,000 over the course of the following month. This was highly unusual, as even though I had earned up to

$20,000 per month from maybe 20-30 traders in the past, to earn such a large amount from one trader so quickly was incredible!

At the time I recognised this as a blessing from God to pay for my business class tickets to Israel!

Five days later on the 29th of May, I departed for Israel.

It wasn't until two and a half years later, while I was out talking to my neighbour, that I would realise the significance of the dates of when I was first given the idea to visit Israel, to the time that I departed.

In a casual conversation with my next-door neighbour, I was explaining to him that it was only three months from getting the idea to visit Israel, to the time that I departed. And that got me thinking, 'how long actually was it from the time that I got the idea to visit Israel, to the time that I departed?'
So I decided to look up my old bank and email records to try and find out.

I had to call the bank to find the old transaction of when I had purchased the travel guide to Israel, on the day I had received the idea. They informed me it was April the 10th, 2010. So I looked up my old email records and found the email to my dad, saying that I was thinking of visiting Israel for the first time on April the 10th, 2010.

From there I was able to deduce that it was exactly *seven weeks to the day* from when I was first given the idea to visit Israel, to the day that I departed!

I was amazed! There it seems, without my knowledge of it, God had been guiding my every step of the way to make sure that He left a sign on this trip, so that I would know that it was Him behind it!

I probably knew this anyway, given how the idea came to me in such an out-of-the-blue type way, however, to have God leave a sign on this trip was no less amazing to me.

So in my mind, I had proof that God was behind this trip.

However, that was not the only sign that He would leave on this trip, but I wouldn't discover this until another five years later!

This would be the first in a series of trips to Israel that God would mark with the number seven.

5. 7 MONTHS

Having sold my website in late 2013, I ran out of money in early 2015. At that point I was intending to get a job, however, it seemed that God had other plans.

Without any income, I had to start living off my credit card, as there were no other options. Before long, I also had to start selling off my assets. I sold my car, and any other item that had any meaningful value. One of those items was my Yamaha T121 piano.

I had bought this piano new in July 2009 for $10,000. The piano was in storage in Whangarei where I had previously lived between May 2010 and January 2012. I had tried selling it online on an auction site several times, but without any luck. Finally I decided that I would take it into the local music shop in Whangarei to sell it. That was in November 2015.

So I flew up to Whangarei and arranged for my piano to be taken from storage and into the music shop. The owner gave me the name of a piano mover to shift it from storage and into the shop.

On November 3, 2015, I arranged for the piano to be taken into the music shop. The first thing that the piano mover said to me when he picked up the phone was, "JESUS LOVES YOU!" I found that quite humorous the way he delivered it over the phone!

So I signed the contract with the music store, and set an asking price of $7,000 for the piano. I flew home the next day and waited until it was sold.

SIX MONTHS LATER IN early May 2016, I suddenly received the idea to visit Israel for a third time.

After selling my website in late 2013, God inspired me to visit Israel for a second time from December 19, 2013, returning on New Year's Eve, December 31, 2013. This covered the Christmas period in Israel, and I visited Bethlehem in the West Bank on Boxing Day (December 26), where Jesus was said to have been born.

For me to be visiting Israel for a third time when I had no money, made absolutely no sense to me! Nevertheless, this seemed to be what God wanted me to do at this time, and so I just had to follow the Spirit where it led me, and see what came of it.

On the 8th of May, I started booking

accommodation online for my trip to Israel, leaving on the 14th of June, and returning on the 30th of June 2016.

For about 10 days I kept getting strong promptings in my spirit to go and book a flight to Israel, however, when I actually came to sit down at my computer and book the ticket, it never felt right! So this didn't make any sense to me. Why would God be prompting me to book a flight to Israel, but then when I sit down to actually book the ticket, He wouldn't open the door for me to do so?

It went on like this for about 10 days until finally, on May 14, 2016, when I sat down at my computer to book the ticket, it finally felt right! So I went ahead and booked a non-refundable economy class ticket to Israel, leaving on the 14th of June from New Zealand, and departing on the 28th of June from Israel. As it happened, it was exactly one month to the day to my departure date on June 14, on the day that I booked these tickets.

There was another interesting aspect to the date that God allowed me to book my flights on, although I didn't discover this until nearly two years later!

In mid-late 2017, while reading a book on the modern history of Israel, I discovered that Israel declared its independence from the British on May 14, 1948! So the date that God allowed me to buy my tickets on, was the anniversary of Israel's independence in 1948! It wasn't until February 2018 while I was writing an article for my website, that I discovered the date that I had bought my tickets on!

It seems that God wanted to leave a sign on this trip to let me know that it was indeed Him behind it! But I knew that already. This was just God's way of proving it.

The fact that I had bought a non-refundable airline ticket only raised the stakes, because at that point, I still didn't know if I would actually end up going to Israel, as I would have to put the entire trip on my credit card, and that didn't make any logical sense whatsoever! So for me, there was still a very real risk that I wouldn't end up going, and I would lose the $2,300 (US$1,500) that I had spent on my airline tickets.

Another interesting aspect of this trip is that I allowed God to design every aspect of it, right down to the flights, accommodation, towns I would visit, and even the sites I would visit. I would wait until He inspired me with any aspect of the trip before writing it down, or acting on anything. That way I knew that He had designed every detail of the trip, and that His will would be done.

At about 7:30PM on the evening of June 3, 2016, exactly seven months to the day that I had brought my piano into the shop to sell it, I suddenly felt compelled to tell my dad that, "it is probably more likely than not that I will be heading to Israel". It wasn't until that very moment that I was fairly certain that I would be heading to Israel, despite my precarious financial situation!

The very next morning on Saturday June 4, I

received a very interesting email. It read, in part:

"Hi Steve
I had some people in late yesterday who'd like to buy your piano.
They've offered $6500.
It's been here a while now, would be good to move it on.
Let me know your thoughts."

Needless to say, I was thrilled! The sale of my piano would fund the majority of my trip to Israel! There was a small amount that would go on my credit card, but the majority of the trip would be funded by the sale of my piano. Had it not been for the fact that God got me to book the King David Hotel in Jerusalem – one of the most expensive and prestigious hotels in all of Israel – maybe all of that trip could have been funded by the sale of my piano.

At that point I still didn't know exactly how long my piano had been in the shop for. I figured it must have been about six months or so. When I went back and had a look at the contract, and realised that it was exactly seven months to the day that I had signed it, to the day that the buyers had come into the shop to buy it, I was amazed!

The buyers had come in at the last possible moment to ensure that there was an exact seven month interval between the time that I brought my piano into the shop, to the time that they came into the shop to buy it! That is God's perfect timing for you! It couldn't have been done any better!

So I departed for Israel on my third trip exactly ten days later on June 14, 2016.

Had God allowed me to get a job when I ran out of money in early 2015 and not go into debt, I wouldn't have had to sell my piano, and therefore, this story would not have happened!

THERE WAS ONE OTHER interesting aspect to this trip that I haven't touched upon.

The very first hotel that God got me to book was the Crowne Plaza Hotel in Tel Aviv city centre. That was on the 8th of May 2016.

Exactly one month later, just days before I was due to depart, there was a terrorist attack on the 8th of June in the Sarona Market, only a five-minute walk from my hotel in Tel Aviv. Two Palestinian terrorists opened fire in a crowded café, killing four people. I wasn't actually due to stay in the hotel until the 24th of June, so it was a long way away still.

While I was in Tel Aviv, I walked over to the café where this happened at around lunchtime, expecting to see the place nearly empty. On the contrary, the place was packed! So it just goes to show you the resilience of the people who endure the daily threat of terrorism, but who just get on with their everyday lives.

This event happening so close to where I was going to be staying might have put some people off, but because I was allowing God to create my itinerary, I trusted Him that everything would work out okay, and of course, it did!

God had now marked two trips with the number seven, separated by exactly six years apart.

I had left Israel on June the 15th, 2010 at around 10PM, and arrived back in Israel on June the 16th, 2016 at about 2AM.

God's timing never ceases to amaze me!

6. 7 YEARS

On the 25th of March 2017, God again moved me to look at booking a trip to Israel for a fourth time. I still had no money, and was still living off my credit card, and so the likelihood of me going to Israel at this point was fairly low!

As soon as the idea came to me, I felt that I should use the El Al website to look at booking a flight, so I sat down at my computer and picked out some dates that I allowed myself to be led to. I felt myself being drawn to the month of May, and ended up picking May the 8th as a departure date from New Zealand, and returning from Israel on May the 27th.

Because I had no way to pay for the tickets or to fund my trip to Israel, I had to discard the booking process.

However, about half an hour later, I found myself wondering about what date that flight arrived back in

New Zealand. Intrigued enough, I came back to my computer and entered in the same departure dates again.

The flight arrived back in New Zealand on the 29th of May – exactly seven years to the day that my first trip departed for Israel back in 2010!

I have no doubt that God was the inspiration behind this trip, because the promptings that I received in my spirit were no different than the ones I received a year earlier, that resulted in my piano taking seven months to the day to sell.

For whatever reason, this trip never eventuated, even though I was inspired to plan out and book the entire trip, except for the flights.

I suspect that had I sold my website at the end of 2009, I would have gone on this trip; however, things didn't work out in the original way that I think they were intended to. Nonetheless, there was one other interesting aspect to this trip that I discovered some time later.

Of the three trips that God had inspired and marked with the number seven; ('7 weeks', '7 months' and '7 years') the first trip began in the Hebrew year 5770, and the last trip would have ended in the Hebrew year 5777! To me that was another clear sign and 'proof' that God was indeed the inspiration behind these trips. I didn't even know that there was such a thing as a Hebrew year until around 2015 or so, five years after my first trip to Israel! So there is absolutely no way that I could have created this in advance of it happening.

What I am clear on though is that if you listen to and obey the Spirit of God, He is able to design and create messages and signs that we can all see.

The fact that I didn't get to go on this trip is not evidence of failure to me, either on my behalf or God's. It is just that He chose not to provide for this trip, even though He inspired it.

I am not privy to the mind of God – none of us are, but we each just have to listen to and follow the Spirit as it is given to us, and let God take care of the outcome. We may not know the outcome in advance, but we still have to follow the Spirit, and God will take care of the rest!

7. 70 YEARS

On February 5, 2018, while lying on my bed, I suddenly received very strong inspiration to book the King David Hotel in Jerusalem. This seemed very unusual, as only the day before I had defaulted on my credit card owing just over $33,000. Still, I tested the Spirit to see if it actually was God who wanted me to do this, and I was certain that this is what He wanted me to do.

No sooner had this idea come to mind, than I thought of May the 14th as the date to make the booking – the 70th anniversary of Israel's independence in 1948! Whether this trip would come about or not, it would mean that God had inspired and marked four different trips over four separate years with the number seven: "7 weeks" in 2010, "7 months" in 2016, "7 years" in 2017 and "70 years" in 2018; with the first three of those trips beginning in the Hebrew year 5770, and ending in the Hebrew year 5777! That seemed more by design than coincidence, and evidence of a pattern that only God could create. In fact, I don't suppose that this pattern could have been created at any other time in history until now! Why else would God want to mark these trips with the number seven, other than to prove that it was Him behind them?

I can see no other reason to do this, other than to prove His existence, and back up what is written in the Bible with its frequent use of the number seven. It is one thing to tell people that you "hear from God", but it is entirely another thing to be able to back it up with evidence! To me, these numbers are God's evidence of design and inspiration. I did not create these patterns myself, I simply responded to the Spirit of God as it moved me to do so. And now, looking back, I can see God's Hand at work guiding my hand at every step of the way, to ensure that His will was accomplished! I have no doubt that it was God behind the inspiration for all of these trips, including my second trip to Israel which wasn't marked by the number seven, but had an important role to play nonetheless. I will get to that later.

It is impossible for me to be able to translate the inspiration that I receive from God to another person, so in the absence of that, there needs to be something else to be able to back up one's claims. For me, that evidence is in the numbers; because that is the way that God is using me to prove my claims!

For other people it may be something else, for instance, with miracle healings the evidence is clear. The person has either been healed or they haven't. With prophecies, either they come true or they don't.

There can be no fudging of the numbers or the truth! They speak for themselves.

So with that in mind, I will get on with the rest of the story.

Following God's prompting, I booked the King David Hotel in Jerusalem from May the 14th to May the 19th, coinciding with the 70th anniversary of Israel's independence on May 14, 2018.

As previously mentioned, the King David Hotel is one of the premier hotels in all of Israel, and one of the most expensive. I think the cheapest room typically sells for around US$500 per night, depending on the season. It has a long and storied history, and was once used by the British as their headquarters during the British Mandate of Palestine, before Israel gained its independence in 1948.

Many world leaders and dignitaries have stayed here over the years, including Winston Churchill, Margaret Thatcher and Barack Obama. I have stayed there twice before, once in 2010 on my first trip and again in 2016 on my third trip to Israel, staying in the southern wing which was once bombed by the Jewish Irgun forces in retaliation against the British in 1946. So for me to be booking this hotel only one day after defaulting on my credit card seemed like absolute lunacy, however, I was certain that this is what God wanted me to do, so I did it. It did not make any sense to me whatsoever!

Still, God has His ways and His means, and they

may not make sense to us at the time, but hopefully with time those things will be revealed to us as to what God's plans were. We just have to trust the Spirit and let God take care of the rest. The outcome is in His hands.

The next day on February 6, God started giving me inspiration for places to visit while I would be in Israel, assuming that I would actually go to Israel!

On previous occasions I have written these down on a piece of paper or added them to a computer document; but this time for whatever reason, I decided to record them in an email that I sent to myself, to record the dates and times that these locations were given to me.

The very first location that I was given to visit was Tel Megiddo, or for those who don't know, the future location of the battle of Armageddon!

I found this quite a provocative first location to give me as a place to visit!

The second location was given to me a few hours later. That location was Masada, an ancient palace-fortress built by King Herod the Great next to the Dead Sea, and the site of a famous last stand by Jewish rebels who were rebelling against Roman rule in approximately 74 A.D.

For the next nearly five weeks, I would write down and record each location in an email sent to myself, as and when the Spirit inspired me with a place to visit.

Here are the remaining places that God inspired me with to visit from February 6 to March 12:

Date	Location	Days
Feb 6	Tel Megiddo	0
Feb 6	Masada	0
Feb 7	City of David	1
Feb 8	King Herod's Palace, Jericho	1
Feb 9	Wadi Qelt	1
Feb 16	Jaffa	7
Feb 23	Mt. Carmel, Haifa	7
Mar 12	Church of the Holy Sepulchre	17

As you can see from the preceding chart, the last place that God inspired me to visit was the Church of the Holy Sepulchre in Jerusalem. When this was given to me, I was briefly reticent to write it down because I wasn't sure if it was an authentic location or not, but the inspiration was strong, and so I wrote it down as a place to visit.

The Church of the Holy Sepulchre is considered to be one of the potential locations of Jesus Christ's crucifixion, burial and resurrection from the dead. It is considered by some to be the 'holiest place in Christianity'. The church complex houses the site of His crucifixion – "Golgotha" or Calvary, as well as the tomb where it is said that Jesus was buried and rose again from the dead, three days later. It was seventeen days since God had given me the last location to write down – Mt. Carmel in Haifa –

before giving me the Church of the Holy Sepulchre as a place to write down.

The length of time between being given these locations to visit was getting longer and longer as time went by, and it would only get longer!

The third column in the preceding chart shows the number of days between each subsequent location that was given to me to write down. It started with two on the first day, then three locations separated by one day each, then two locations separated by seven days each, and then finally one location separated by seventeen days – the Church of the Holy Sepulchre.

Some say that Jesus Christ rose from the dead on the 17th day of the Jewish month of Nisan, so maybe God was giving me a sign here by attaching 17 days to the Church of the Holy Sepulchre, where it is said that Jesus rose from the dead! Just a thought.

The two locations separated by seven days each is also intriguing to me, although I have yet to figure out if there is any significance to it. Jaffa is an ancient port in Israel just south of Tel Aviv where Jonah embarked on his ill-fated voyage from, and it is also where St. Peter the apostle had his famous vision that the Gentiles were no longer to be considered "unclean". It is also the port where King Solomon received the Cedars from Lebanon to build the first Jewish Temple.

Mt. Carmel in Haifa is the place where the prophet Elijah is said to have spent some time in a cave. He is well known for destroying the prophets of Baal, an ancient pagan religion in 1 Kings 18:20.

So whether these two locations being separated by seven days each has any hidden meaning, I have yet to find out.

In any case, after God gave me the Church of the Holy Sepulchre to write down on the 12th of March 2018, everything went quiet. It seemed as if something had happened and I would not be going to Israel after all, even if it was possible for me to do so at the time! Weeks went by and nothing happened. No more inspiration about places to visit or write down, it all seemingly went dead.

That was until the 1st of May!

While I was sitting on a recliner watching TV at about 5:38PM, I suddenly received inspiration to visit the Garden Tomb in Jerusalem! It was a complete bolt out of the blue as if it came from nowhere! But it was also very clear. So I got up, sat down at my computer, and wrote it down in the old email that I had been sending myself.

It had been so long since I had been inspired with a place to visit, that I had to scroll through weeks of emails just to try and find it! When I did, I saw that the date that the last location was given to me was on the 12th of March. That immediately got me thinking exactly how long it had been between the last two locations that God had given to me. The answer was exactly 50 days!

Now from my brief understanding of Judaism, I knew that that was an important number for the Jews, but only so far as it related to the Jubilee year held every 50 years, in which all debts were cancelled. I wasn't aware of any other meaning to the number.

So after a quick Google search, I discovered something very interesting indeed!

In Judaism, the Jews are instructed to number fifty days between the "Feast of First Fruits" and the "Feast of Weeks", also known as "Shavuot" in Hebrew, or "Pentecost" in Christianity. "Pentecost" comes from the Greek word for "fiftieth".
So that's when I realised something else.

The Garden Tomb in Jerusalem is a competing location for the burial and resurrection of Jesus Christ. In the New Testament, the apostle Paul describes Jesus Christ as the "firstfruits" from the dead. (See 1 Corinthians 15:20). So then I realised the significance of what God had just done!

He had separated the two locations associated with the resurrection of Jesus Christ as the "firstfruits" from the dead by exactly fifty days – the length of time that God instructed the Jews to count between the "Feast of First Fruits" and the "Feast of Weeks" exactly fifty days later! In Judaism, this is called the "Counting of the Omer", and it is still observed today.

I was amazed! God had just verified a part of the Bible by using two popular locations that are generally accepted as potential locations for the resurrection of Jesus Christ from the dead, using some scripture that is believed to have been written by Moses about 3,500 years ago! The fulfilment of the "Feast of Weeks" or Shavuot, was in the coming of the Holy Spirit in Acts 2:1-4, fifty days after Christ's resurrection as the "firstfruits" from the dead!

There was another interesting aspect to this story that I discovered just over two months later.

Back on December 23, 2017, I had purchased a book called *"The Holy Land for Christian Travelers"* by John A. Beck. I never got around to reading this book, so it just sat in my pile of books to read!

Then, two months after this story happened, on July 10, 2018, I felt that God wanted me to add this book to my website. So I did. The next day, I felt God prompting me to pick up the book and have a look through it. I wasn't sure what I was supposed to be looking at, so I just had a quick skim through various parts of the book. As I was about to put it down, I discovered some suggested itineraries at the front of the book. John suggests three itineraries for 3, 5 and 12-day trips to Jerusalem and Israel. Then I discovered what God had wanted me to see!

Each one of these itineraries starts with a visit to the Church of the Holy Sepulchre, followed by a trip to the Garden Tomb! All that time that book had been sitting there, waiting for me to read it, and discover the connection between my story that God had created, and the suggested itineraries that were provided in this book! God certainly knows the future in advance, and how to create signs that back up and verify the things that He has done!

THERE WAS ONE FINAL aspect to this story regarding the timing of the dates that these locations were given to me. Interestingly, the Garden Tomb was given to me exactly twelve weeks to the day from the first location on February 6!

For those that don't know, the number twelve plays an important role in scripture. There were twelve tribes of Israel: Reuben, Simeon, Levi, Judah, Dan, Naphtali, Gad, Asher, Issachar, Zebulun, Joseph & Benjamin; there were twelve apostles of Jesus Christ; there are 12,000 saints from each of the twelve tribes of Israel, making up the 144,000 saints of Revelation 7:4; and twelve gates in the new Jerusalem, each having the name of one of the twelve tribes of Israel. (Revelation 21:12).

So for me, the fact that the Garden Tomb was given to me exactly twelve weeks to the day since the first location, is evidence of design, not coincidence.

For the record, there were three other locations that were given to me after the Garden Tomb. They were: the Church of the Annunciation in Nazareth on May 2; Yardenit on the Jordan River on May 7; and the Sea of Galilee on May 26; bringing the total number of locations that God gave to me to write down to twelve. Once again, I don't think that that was an accident! Twelve locations with the most important one coming exactly twelve weeks to the day from being given the first one. But I will leave that up to the reader to decide on that!

The last three locations all had significant meaning in the life of Jesus. The Basilica of the Annunciation in Nazareth is where tradition holds that the archangel Gabriel appeared to Mary, the mother of Jesus, to announce that she would bear a child – Jesus, the Son of God.

Yardenit is a location on the Jordan River, in which Jesus was baptised by John the Baptist. Although not considered the authentic location of his baptism, it does commemorate the baptism of Jesus in the Jordan River.

The twelfth and final location given to me was the Sea of Galilee in the north of Israel. This is where Jesus lived and carried out a large part of His ministry from the time He was baptised.

8. CLOSING ARGUMENTS

On the 5th of May 2018, exactly three months to the day that God first inspired me to book the King David Hotel in Jerusalem, He prompted me to cancel the trip! Once again, the evidence of His timing is so precise in that it was exactly three months to the day since He first inspired me with the idea to go. It wasn't until after I started cancelling the bookings that I realised that it was exactly three months to the day.

God never had any intention of sending me to Israel for a fourth time, He was simply finishing a story that He had started to write back in 2010 on my first trip to Israel!

All throughout this trip is evidence of design; not by me, but from God.

It was exactly fourteen weeks to the day from when I was first inspired to book the King David

Hotel, to the 14th of May when I would check in to the hotel on Israel's 70th anniversary of their independence in 1948. Everything was precisely timed and designed to show the Hand of God at work! As it says in the book of Proverbs:

"It is the glory of God to conceal a thing: but the honour of kings is to search out a matter." – Proverbs 25:2

God conceals things in order for them to be revealed in their due time, but not before.

He used those three months to tell a story that would reveal certain things at a certain time. Things about which I didn't know much about before they were revealed to me! In fact, I will give you an example.

On the 17th of May 2018, I felt God prompting me to buy a book on the feasts of Israel, about which I didn't know much about at the time. That was sixteen days after God had revealed to me the meaning behind the fifty days between the Church of the Holy Sepulchre and the Garden Tomb.

So I ended up buying a book called *"The Feasts of Israel"* by Dr. Chuck Missler, whose work I had come across before. As it turned out, Dr. Missler had died sixteen days earlier on the 1st of May – the same day that God had given me the Garden Tomb as a place to visit after the fifty day period. However, what I was to find in that book was much more interesting!

I said earlier in this book that God had left another

sign on my first trip to Israel that I didn't discover until eight years after I got back. According to Dr. Missler's book, Jesus Christ entered Jerusalem on the back of a donkey presenting Himself as the Messiah on April 6, 32 A.D. That equated to the 10th day of Nisan on the Jewish calendar, where Jews are required to present an unblemished lamb to the temple for inspection. Jesus Christ is that unblemished lamb.

Four days later on the 14th day of Nisan, they are required to slaughter it. This is a model of what was to happen to Jesus Christ when He was crucified. The unblemished lamb who would be slaughtered to take away the sins of the world. Jesus was the Passover lamb – one of the seven feasts of Moses.

If Dr. Missler's calculation and interpretation is correct, that would mean that Jesus Christ was crucified on the 10th of April, 32 A.D., at approximately 33 years of age. What was interesting about that for me was that I was exactly 33 years and 33 days old on the 10th of April 2010, on the very day that God inspired me to visit Israel for the first time, 1,978 years to the day that Jesus Christ was crucified on the cross in Jerusalem. So that was quite an incredible discovery! Interestingly, the vote to create Israel in the United Nations also passed by exactly 33 votes on November 29, 1947. And, believe it or not, November 29 is the 333rd day of the year!

Another interesting aspect about the number 33, is that King David reigned over Israel from Jerusalem for 33 years, and Jesus is a descendant from the line of David.

Had I bought any other book on the feasts of Israel, I would have no doubt not discovered this link to my first trip to Israel, eight years earlier. That trip departed for Israel exactly *seven weeks later to the day* on May 29, 2010, beginning a series of trips that God would mark with the number seven!

So everything is revealed in its due time, but not before.

Had God not prompted me to buy a book on the feasts of Israel, I would be none the wiser about the meaning behind the date of when I was first inspired to visit Israel. The fact that I was exactly 33 years and 33 days old on that date, only goes to reinforce the point that this series of trips was God designed, and God-inspired. I could not have created this pattern even if I tried! I am not that smart enough, and no one lives their lives trying to mould it to numbers and patterns that they know nothing about! This was something that God had decided to do for me, for whatever reason, to try and prove His existence and prove the presence of His divinely guiding hand in all that we do!

70 Days

There was one other interesting point to this series of trips that I haven't touched upon yet.

On the 8th of May 2018, I discovered that if I add up all the days that I have spent in Israel, including all the days from the series of trips that God had inspired and marked with the number seven, i.e. "7 weeks", "7 months", "7 years" and "70 years", they all add up to exactly 70 days!

That is not a coincidence! 70 is a very significant number in Israel's history throughout the Bible, and so again, given all the signs and numbers that God has used throughout this series of trips, this must be by design, not coincidence.

So the series of trips that began with the "7 week" trip and ended with the "70 year" trip, including my second trip that was not marked by the number seven, all added up to exactly 70 days! I mentioned earlier that my second trip to Israel played an important role in this series of trips, even though it wasn't marked by the number seven, and this is why. It was used to make up the numbers to add up to exactly 70 days!

The following chart shows the number of days that I have spent in Israel, including those trips that God inspired and marked with the number seven. I didn't get to go on all of them, but they were all inspired by God. And to me, this is proof of that!

Trip	Dates	Days
"7 Weeks"	May 31-Jun 15, 2010	16
Christmas	Dec 21-29, 2013	9
"7 Months"	Jun 16-28, 2016	13
"7 Years"	May 10-27, 2017	18
"70 Years"	May 14-27, 2018	14
	TOTAL	**70**

9. 12 WEEKS

On October 20, 2018, God inspired me to book another trip to Israel. I still didn't have the money to be able to go, however, I went ahead and booked the trip anyway – everything except the flights, which would have actually cost me money to be able to book!

I ended up picking a departure date of January 14, 2019 from New Zealand, and returning on January 28 from Israel. As it happened, these dates were exactly two years and seven months to the day since the last trip that I actually went on in June 2016. That trip was characterised by "7 months", in that it took exactly seven months to the day from the time I brought my piano into the shop to sell it, to the day that the buyers came into the shop to buy it!

As with previous trips, I decided to let God build the trip for me, by waiting until He inspired me with any aspect of the trip before writing it down or acting on anything. Here is the full itinerary for the trip:

Date	Location	Hotel
Jan 14, 2019	Depart N.Z.	-
Jan 15-19	Jerusalem	King David
Jan 19-23	Jericho	Oasis
Jan 23-24	Be'er Sheva	Leonardo
Jan 24-25	Nazareth	Golden Crown
Jan 25-27	Tiberias	Scots
Jan 27-28	Jaffa	Market House
Jan 28	Depart Israel	-

Locations:

Nazareth

- Mt. Precipice
- Mt. Tabor
- Mensa Christi Church

Jerusalem

- The Davidson Centre & Archaeological Park
- Church of the Holy Sepulchre
- Mt. of Olives
- Pools of Bethesda
- Hinnom Valley
- Western Wall
- Mary's Tomb
- Garden Tomb

- Temple Mount

Jericho

- Wadi Qelt
- Ein Gedi
- Ein Prat Spring
- Mt. of Temptation
- Tel es-Sultan
- Dead Sea
- Masada
- Ein es-Sultan

Nablus

- Sebastia
- Jacob's Well

Tiberias

- Mt. of the Beatitudes
- Capernaum
- Mt. Carmel
- Caesarea
- Beit She'an
- Ein Tabgha

Bethlehem

- Herodion
- Church of the Nativity

Hebron

• Tomb of the Patriarchs

Tel Aviv

• Jaffa

These locations were given to me over a three month period starting on October 22, 2018. The towns are in the order that they were given to me, and the locations within those towns are in the order that they were given to me.

With only two days left until my departure date on January 14, 2019, I decided to look up the weekly Torah portion on the day that God inspired me to book the trip. Because I was inspired to book this trip on the Sabbath day (Saturday), I was wondering whether there might be a message in that. It turns out that there was!

It was Saturday the 12th of January, 2019, when I decided to look up the weekly Torah portion on the day that God inspired me to book the trip. It was exactly 12 weeks to the day since that date on October 20, 2018.

Jews read the first five books of the Bible, otherwise known as the "Torah", in weekly portions throughout the year. They have been doing this for thousands of years. Some say that Moses instituted it, while others say that Ezra the Scribe instituted it after his return from Babylon in the 5th Century B.C.

It turns out that the weekly Torah portion on the day that God inspired me to book this trip, begins with one of the most seminal events in Israel's history!

Here is the exact quote:

"Now the LORD had said unto Abram, Get thee out of thy country, and from thy kindred, and from thy father's house, unto a land that I will shew thee:" – Genesis 12:1

Amazingly, the day that I discovered this had the same number as the verse! 12 January or 12/1, and Genesis 12:1. The Torah portions fall on different days each year, so in most other years, 12 weeks from this Torah portion would not have landed on the 12th of January at all! This again is evidence of God's timing at work.

The name of this Torah portion on October 20, 2018, is called "Parashat Lech-lecha", which means "go" in Hebrew. The Torah portions are named after the first significant word in the text, which in this case is "go".

So here it was, exactly twelve weeks to the day that God had inspired me to "go" to Israel, and the Torah portion seemed to be calling me to visit Israel once again! "Get out of your country, and from your people, and from your father's house, to a land that I will show you!"

The fact that I lived with my father at the time only made the verse even more apt! In this verse,

God is telling Abraham to leave his home country in Mesopotamia (modern-day Iraq/Turkey) and go to a land that He will show him – the land of Israel. Abraham is the father of the Jewish people, through Isaac, Jacob and Jacob's twelve sons, who would later make up the twelve tribes of Israel. As you can see, the number twelve plays a very important role in Israel's history.

The last part of this discovery is that the Torah portion that fell on the 12th of January, 2019, is called "Parashat Bo", which also means "go" or "come" in Hebrew. So there are two Torah portions separated by exactly twelve weeks apart that are both named by the Hebrew word for "go". It just so happens that the first one also fell on the same day that God inspired me to book this trip to Israel!

Earlier in this book I wrote about how God gave me twelve locations to visit, and the most important one was given to me exactly twelve weeks to the day from the first one. I said I would leave it up to the reader to decide whether they thought this was God's work or not. It now seems clear to me that God indeed had His hand on this, and that being given twelve locations with the most important one coming exactly twelve weeks to the day from the first one, wasn't an accident at all! It is very clear evidence of God's Hand at work as the source, inspiration and power behind all these trips to Israel.

There was one final aspect to this trip that I haven't touched upon yet.

Though God did not provide the money for me to go on this trip, I discovered another very interesting 'sign' that God left on this trip, so that I would know that it was Him behind it!

On January 31, 2019, the day after this trip was due to get back to New Zealand, I realised that if I added up all the days I was due to spend in Israel, together with the days from the previous trips, they all added up to exactly 84 days or 12 weeks!

So yet again, God had one last 'sign' to leave on this trip for all of our benefit!

Here now is an updated table showing the latest "12 week" trip added:

Trip	Dates	Days
"7 Weeks"	May 31-Jun 15, 2010	16
Christmas	Dec 21-29, 2013	9
"7 Months"	Jun 16-28, 2016	13
"7 Years"	May 10-27, 2017	18
"70 Years"	May 14-27, 2018	14
"12 Weeks"	Jan 15-28, 2019	14
	TOTAL	**84**

❖ ❖ ❖

Second "12 Week" Trip

Six weeks later on March 17, 2019 (St. Patrick's Day), God put a location inside my head called "Yardenit" in Israel. Yardenit is a baptismal site located on the Jordan River just south of the Sea of Galilee. As mentioned earlier, it is not considered the authentic location of Jesus's baptism, although it does commemorate his baptism in the Jordan River.

Despite becoming a Christian more than twenty years ago, I still have not been baptised! Something of an oversight I know, however, I have just not got around to doing it yet!

So my immediate thoughts upon receiving this strong inspiration of Yardenit in my spirit, was that maybe God wanted me to be baptised at this location in Israel. Soon after, I went online and decided to pick out some dates for another potential trip to Israel. I ended up picking a departure date of the 13th of June, 2019 from New Zealand, and returning on the 26th of June from Israel.

Two hours later I was doing some mental arithmetic in my head, and worked out that it was 88 days from today's date until my proposed departure date. That works out to be twelve weeks and four days.

And then I discovered something interesting!

The Feast of Weeks/Shavuot and Pentecost, all fall on the 9th of June – exactly twelve weeks from today's date!

So that is now four times that God has used the time period of 'twelve weeks' in a row! What's more is that the first time He used it, it was used to mark the end of a fifty-day period that Jews are told to count between the Feast of First Fruits and the Feast of Weeks, fifty-days later!

Another thing I discovered was that my departure date comes exactly twelve weeks to the day from the Jewish holiday of "Purim" on March 21, 2019. Purim celebrates the deliverance of the Jews from the Persian ruler, Haman, who was planning to kill all the Jews. This story is covered in the biblical book of Esther.

Purim is held on the 14th of the Hebrew month of Adar, however, in a Hebrew leap year such as this one, it is celebrated on the 14th of Adar II – the thirteenth month in the Hebrew calendar.

So for me, this again is proof that God is guiding my hand, thoughts and spirit in everything that I do!

Whether I actually end up going on this trip is another matter, but what I have realised is that it's not always about the act of going, but rather the story that God creates around the idea of going!

10. DONALD TRUMP & THE NUMBER 7

How could any self-respecting book not include something about Donald Trump if it wanted to sell copies?! God only knows how much money has been made off selling books related to Donald Trump and their associated media. However, this chapter is not about exploiting Donald Trump, it is about drawing attention to an incredible series of 'coincidences' that relate to Donald Trump, Israel and the number seven.

Here is a list of some of those incredible 'coincidences'.

- On Donald Trump's first full day in office, he was exactly 70 years, 7 months and 7 days old. He was born exactly 700 days before Israel gained its independence on May 14, 1948.

- He was elected on Prime Minister Benjamin Netanyahu's 7th year, 7th month and 7th full day in office. Prime Minister Netanyahu has been the current Prime Minister of Israel since March 31, 2009. He was sworn in just before midnight on March 31, 2009, so his first full day in office was on April 1, 2009. Donald Trump was elected on November 8, 2016, 7 years, 7 months and 7 days later!

- Exactly 7 months to the day from Donald Trump's first full day in office on January 21, 2017, a total solar eclipse occurred – the first to be seen exclusively in the United States since before the nation was founded in 1776.

- He beat Hillary Clinton by exactly 77 votes in the Electoral College voting system, as a result of 7 "faithless" voters who chose not to vote for the candidate they were pledged to vote for. Two Electoral College members voted against Donald Trump, while five voted against Hillary Clinton, bringing the final tally to 304-227 votes.

- On 7/7/17, Donald Trump met with Russian President Vladimir Putin for the first time face-to-face when Vladimir Putin was exactly 777 months old to the day. He was born on October 7, 1952.

- All these events occurred in the Hebrew year, 5777. (Except for Donald Trump's birth date.)

- In the 77th week since Donald Trump's inauguration, he was listed by Forbes' real-time billionaires list as the 777th richest person in the world!

Can all this be a coincidence? Or is there something else more interesting going on here? I will attempt to figure it out.

For most Christians, we believe that presidents, prime ministers and other global leaders are divinely appointed by God. Even the King of Babylon, Nebuchadnezzar declared as much:

"This matter is by the decree of the watchers, and the demand by the word of the holy ones: to the intent that the living may know that the most High ruleth in the kingdom of men, and giveth it to whomsoever he will, and setteth up over it the basest of men." – Daniel 4:17

To be clear, I am not calling Donald Trump "the basest of men" here, I am simply pointing out that it is the divinely appointed will of God as to whom becomes the leader of a country or not. For my part, I never believed that Hillary Clinton would become the president, and my instinct was correct. The only time I wavered was right before the election when all the polls were against Donald Trump, and I figured that my instinct must have been wrong. It wasn't. Always stick with your first instinct! It is probably correct.

Now since Donald Trump has been elected, some interesting things have happened.

On December 6, 2017, 70 years and 7 days since the State of Israel was created in the United Nations by a resolution to partition Palestine, Donald Trump announced that the United States would recognise Jerusalem as Israel's capital, and move the United States Embassy to Jerusalem. Furthermore, they later announced that the embassy would open on Israel's 70th anniversary of its independence on May 14, 1948!

The vote in the United Nations to partition Palestine came on November 29, 1947, just five months earlier. The United States subsequently opened their embassy on May 14, 2018, 70 years to the hour that soon-to-be Prime Minister David Ben-Gurion stood up to read out the declaration of independence 70 years earlier.

As mentioned previously, the number 70 has played an important role throughout Israel's history.

In the book of Daniel, he is given a prophecy pertaining to "70 weeks" to usher in the Messiah. Also, in the same book, he recognises the fact that Israel would be in captivity for 70 years in Babylon, according to the prophet Jeremiah. Sadly for the Jews, the second temple was also destroyed by the Romans in Jerusalem in the year 70 A.D., effectively beginning what would be a two-thousand year period of exile from the land. That all came to an end following World War Two and the creation of the state of Israel nearly two-thousand years later.

Jesus Himself predicted that this would happen because the Jewish leadership failed to recognise Him at the hour of His coming:

"And shall lay thee even with the ground, and thy children within thee; and they shall not leave in thee one stone upon another; because thou knewest not the time of thy visitation." – Luke 19:44

Also interesting to note is that both North and South Korea will mark their 70-year anniversaries in 2018, in September and August respectively. North Korea turns 70 years old on September 9, 2018. As it happens, the Jewish New Year will also begin on the evening of September 9, 2018, in the Hebrew year 5779.

Now what all this means for Donald Trump, Israel and the world is anybody's guess. It could mean nothing, and it could mean that God is leaving signs on Donald Trump's presidency to let people know that He is in control. Either way, we won't really know until Donald Trump's presidency comes to an end, or events make it clear as to why Donald Trump was elected! I think we have already seen some of the reasons as to why he was elected, but only time will tell.

Second Edition Update:

Several months after publishing the first edition of this book in October 2018, some more interesting events popped up relating to Donald Trump, Israel and the number seven.

In an odd little reversal of earlier events, (Donald

Trump being born 700 days before Israel was founded, and being inaugurated on his 70th year, 7th month and 7th day of life), James Mattis, Donald Trump's defense secretary, resigned on his and Donald Trump's 700th day in office on December 20, 2018, U.S. time.

Donald Trump made the announcement on Twitter at exactly 5:21 P.M. Eastern Standard Time, which equated to 12:21 A.M. Israeli time on 21/12 – the day that Israel turned 70 years, 7 months and 7 days old!

This was deemed to be a significant event in Donald Trump's administration by many commentators, although what it actually means remains to be seen. That's what I mean by a 'reversal of events', in that significant events occurred at each of these milestones in Donald Trump's life.

Furthermore, James (Jim) Mattis originally set a departure date of February 28, 2019, exactly 70 days from the announcement of his resignation! February 28 would mark both Donald Trump's and Jim Mattis's 770th day in office, as they were both sworn in on the same day.

According to some in the media, because of the coverage that Jim Mattis was receiving in the media, Donald Trump moved forward the departure date of Jim Mattis to January 1, 2019, with acting Secretary of Defense, Patrick Shanahan, to take over from that date.

However, that was not the only interesting event to happen with regards to Donald Trump and Israel.

Only four days later on December 24, 2018, on the 777th day since Donald Trump's election victory on November 8, 2016, Israel's Prime Minister, Benjamin Netanyahu, announced that Israel would be dissolving their parliament and holding early elections in April 2019, approximately seven months earlier than their term would allow. The date for that election has since been set at April 9, 2019. The election must have been held by November 5, 2019.

Then, just 66 days later on February 28, 2019, on Donald Trump's 770th day in office, Israel's attorney general, Avichai Mandelblit, announced that Prime Minister Benjamin Netanyahu will be charged with bribery, fraud and breach of trust charges, pending a hearing. The announcement came after a more than two-year investigation into the matter, and was made exactly 40 days before Israel's general election on April 9, 2019. It marks the first time in Israel's history that a sitting Prime Minister is facing criminal charges.

Then, just three weeks later on the 21st of March, at exactly 12:50 P.M. EDT, on the day that Israel celebrates Purim, Donald Trump announced that it was time to recognise Israel's sovereignty over the Golan Heights. This is a disputed area, much like the West Bank, and was captured by Israel during the Six-Day War in 1967. Earlier in the day, U.S. Secretary of State, Mike Pompeo, himself a Christian, visited the Western Wall with Prime Minister Netanyahu – the first time that America's top diplomat has done so, while being accompanied by a senior Israeli official.

In an interview with CBN, Pompeo agreed that it was possible that God had raised up Donald Trump to defend Israel from Iran – the modern-day Persia – much like the story of Purim in the biblical book of Esther. Pompeo is serving as the 70th United States Secretary of State.

Now again, what all this means for the United States and/or Israel – if anything, is anybody's guess. We will all just have to wait and see!

❖ ❖ ❖

Incidentally, my younger brother Tim was killed on Donald Trump's 63rd birthday in Michigan, USA, in 2009, meaning that he died exactly 7 years, 7 months and 7 days before Donald Trump's first full day in office on January 21, 2017. He was 29 years old.

11. MESSAGES FROM GOD: LIFE AFTER DEATH

On June 14, 2009, my younger brother Tim was killed in a gliding accident near Pinckney, Michigan, USA, where he was living and working at the time.

He was a helicopter pilot for an air ambulance service called MidWest MedFlight, now no longer in operation. He was due to get the nod for 'lead pilot' for the company the day after he died. He was 29 years old.

The day he died, he was taking a trial flight in a glider to see if he wanted to learn how to fly one. It was his first ever, and last ever flight in a glider.

The crash occurred at approximately 11:20AM on a Sunday morning at a place called Richmond Field near Gregory township in Michigan. Tim had been living in Michigan for many years, after leaving New

Zealand to join the French Foreign Legion in France back in 1998 when he was 18 years old. Luckily he was talked out of it by my older brother and his friends while staying in London, U.K., and eventually made his way to Louisiana, USA, to take up an offer of an apprenticeship aircraft mechanic, in exchange for free helicopter flying lessons.

So that is how he became a helicopter pilot. He had about 3,000 flying hours when he died, and was an FAA qualified airframe and power plant mechanic as well. He was working for one of the largest helicopter companies in the world at the time of his death, PHI, Inc, who contracted out their services to MidWest MedFlight. He was stationed at the St. Joseph Mercy Hospital in Ann Arbor, Michigan, when he died.

The timing of his death came as a complete shock to us all. We simply found out by a call from his girlfriend at the time, who rang my dad, who then called me to let me know of his untimely death. It was 8:20AM in the morning on June 15, New Zealand time when I found out. I was shocked! It had come completely out of the blue, although in retrospect, there were some things that led up to his death that appeared to be God preparing us for this tragic event.

Exactly six weeks earlier to the day that Tim was killed, on May 4, 2009, God put it in my heart to buy my first suit. I worked from home at the time, and didn't actually need a suit as far as I was aware, but the prompting seemed insistent, so I ended up buying my first suit on May 4. I probably spent around

$1,500-$2,000 on the suit and accessories, and bought a second suit some weeks later.

Money was not an issue for me at the time, having had my best ever month in revenue a couple of months earlier, receiving about $60,000 in cash to my account in the month of March. The average annual salary in New Zealand at the time was about $50,000.

I was so perplexed as to why I had bought this suit, that I remember telling my dad at the time, "I hope I haven't bought this for your funeral!" It seemed that I had bought it for a reason, but, at the time, I didn't know what it was for. That became clear exactly six weeks later to the day that I bought it.

There were some other smaller warning signs that something might be about to happen, although I didn't recognise these as such at the time.

Tim had posted a picture of his new motorbike on Facebook on May 26, 2009, less than three weeks before his death, and as soon as I saw it, I was so disturbed that I said out loud, "Rest in Peace, Tim". It was quite unusual for me to have that kind of reaction to simply seeing a picture of his new motorbike, as he had owned and ridden a high-performance bike before when he was 17 years old; so it wasn't as if this was anything new to him. So I think my reaction was more to do with what was coming, rather than the motorbike itself. A kind of premonition, if you will.

A few days later he posted another picture of his new bike outside the general store in Hell, Michigan, about seven miles from where he was living in Pinckney! It was entitled, "To HELL and back!"

Also in late May, I woke up feeling really bad about Tim for whatever reason, something I have never felt before. I didn't know what the problem was, but again, I now put this down to some sort of premonition about what was about to happen. Tim had also bought his first suit around the same time as I did, in preparation for his new role as "lead pilot".

My mother also had a dream in early June in which her late mother came to her and gave her a big hug, saying, "You're going to need this, Marion". So, all in all, there were these little warning signs and preparation for an event that was going to happen, but yet we didn't know anything about. Essentially, what that means is that God knew it was going to happen, and He was preparing us for what was about to happen in His own way. He obviously could have stopped it from happening, but that wasn't His will.

So on June 14, 2009, Eastern United States time, Tim was killed in a gliding accident. Because he was sitting in the front seat, in front of the pilot, he took the brunt of the impact when it nose-dived into the ground, following a wing stall.

What that means is that the glider ran out of speed following a turn back to the airfield, and could no longer sustain flight. What happened is that the winch cable that was towing the glider into the sky from the ground, snapped, and because the glider hadn't yet got enough height to make it safely back to the ground, it wasn't able to make a safe return back to the grass landing strip. Therefore, it stalled, and crashed. Tim was killed instantly so it seems, although paramedics worked on him for 45 minutes before pronouncing him dead.

The pilot survived, although spent many months in hospital recovering from multiple injuries, including a spinal injury. He was lucky! We bear no animosity towards him for what happened, it is just one of those things that happens from time to time.

Following the accident, me, Dad, and my older brother David, all made our way over to the funeral held in Dexter, Michigan.

The funeral was held in an old church that was used for the filming of a movie called "Conviction", starring Hilary Swank several months earlier. Tim wasn't a Catholic, but his girlfriend was, and this was part of the congregation that they were attending before he died.

We didn't actually know what Tim's spiritual beliefs were, as we weren't raised in a particularly religious household; although we did have some exposure to Christianity through maybe, 1-2 years of Sunday School, some Christian camps, and religious instruction at school. So it was comforting to hear that he had attended church with his girlfriend!

The suit that I had bought just over seven weeks earlier at God's prompting, I wore to Tim's funeral. That was the reason that God had prompted me to buy it!

The fact that it was just over seven weeks since I had bought it, appeared to be evidence of God's timing for an event that He knew was coming.

At the funeral, one of the songs that was performed was called "Angel", by Sarah McLachlan, sung by three of Tim's girlfriend's nieces. It was sung unaccompanied, 'a capella' style. It was very moving and very beautiful. The song includes the lyrics, "You are pulled from the wreckage", which in Tim's case, was quite apt.

Tim was born on September 9, 1979, and died three months short of his 30th birthday. Nearly four years after his death on April 2, 2013, I came across the official video for the song "Angel", by Sarah McLachlan. Amazingly, this video was uploaded on September 9, 2008 – the date of Tim's last birthday before he died!

It currently has nearly 40 million views as of the time of writing on September 3, 2018.

Here is the link to it:

https://www.youtube.com/watch?v=i1GmxMTwUgs

❖ ❖ ❖

FIRST MESSAGE

On the day of Tim's funeral, inspired by a story of a man who asked God about his dad's final destiny, Dad decided to ask God about Tim's final destiny. That night, unbeknownst to me and my older brother David, Dad made a prayer to God to ask about what happened to Tim.

Two days later he would have his answer!

On Thursday June 25th, David returned to the U.K. where he was living, leaving just me and Dad in the motel in Michigan. I had spotted some advertising leaflets in the motel room earlier that week, advertising various takeaway restaurants in the area. One of them was for the China Garden restaurant in Whitmore Lake where we were staying.

That night we decided to get Chinese takeaways for dinner from the China Garden restaurant. We had to walk about ten minutes across the highway to get our meal. With that meal came two complimentary fortune cookies! I don't think I had ever had a fortune cookie before, at least not as far as I can remember. Mine wasn't particularly interesting, but Dad's one said, "It is given to you to discern higher truths", which he thought was a little pretentious! Nevertheless, the meal was good, and the fortune cookies provided a little bit of interest to the meal. However, Dad's fortune cookie was to play a greater role than he or we thought.

Later that night, at about 3:20AM, Dad would receive an answer to his prayer that he had asked God about Tim's final destiny. I will let him finish the story in his own words:

"That night I awoke in complete darkness (no window in my room) with a message in front of me that was typed on a strip of paper, which later on, I recognised as being similar to the 'fortune cookie' strip I had received the night previously. All it said, quite simply, was that 'The Road to Milford Sound is Open'.

I puzzled about this strange message, which had no resemblance to anything I had dreamed that night – if in fact I had dreamed at all, so, well, it just puzzled me.........Then I thought about Milford Sound, where I had once spent several weeks at the Milford Hotel as it then was in the 1960s, at the time of the summer season where my job was to fly guests from the airstrip on various scenic flights or wherever they wished to go.

For the whole time I was there, the weather was absolutely perfect. I would get up early in the cool of the morning and make sure that my aircraft was ready to fly immediately after breakfast. 'The most beautiful scenic flights in the world' and similar claims – how people would declare the scenery at Milford Sound. As being 'out of this world.'

As early as 100 years ago, some described it as a 'Paradise.' With sudden amazement I translated the message as 'The road to Paradise is open'.

Turning over I looked at the illuminated alarm clock – only 3.32am! Suddenly it hit me – perhaps 10 minutes ago I had become aware of the strange message and this brought the time back to about 3.20 am. This was the time in NZ when Tim had died (instantly it seems) and in the U.S at that time it was 11.20am."

So with that, Dad had an answer to his prayer about how Tim was. He was in heaven with God. The "higher truth" that God had given Dad to "discern", was the message written on the fortune cookie strip, "The Road to Milford Sound is Open".

There was a 50:50 chance that I could have got Dad's fortune cookie, and then the story wouldn't have worked. In response to Dad's prayer about Tim's final destiny, he got the fortune cookie he was meant to receive!

This would be the first in a series of messages we would receive about how Tim was, in response to various people's emotional needs.

It would be another five months before I would receive one myself.

SECOND MESSAGE

S ome months after Tim's death, I was still struggling with his death and wondering what happened to him after he died. I needed confirmation, although I didn't verbalise it to God. I was just worried. God knows the hearts and minds of all people, and knows how to craft a message that speaks directly to that person. This is what happened to me.

On December 2, 2009, while I was driving home from the airport, I noticed a motorbike parked on the side of the road that looked exactly like Tim's. It was! It was a Triumph Daytona motorbike – not a common bike at the best of times, but particularly in a small town the size of 6,000 people! I thought that was quite a neat coincidence.

I told my dad about it and he went down and had a look at it.

About half an hour later as he was getting out of the car, a very low flying helicopter flew over the house on a grey and rainy day. It was very low and very noisy, lower than I had ever seen a helicopter, or any aircraft for that matter, fly over the house before. It made quite an impression on me! It certainly got our attention! No doubt it was flying low to stay under the cloud.

As we walked inside, I mentioned that that was 'two things' relating to Tim, happening in very quick succession. I didn't think anything more of it until later that night, when I was getting ready for bed.

It suddenly hit me that these two events were a message from God, and at that moment, I felt 99% of my sadness lift from me, and I was happy again! The message that I received in my heart was, 'Don't worry, everything's okay'. And I felt such a huge sense of comfort and relief that Tim was okay!

Some time later I remembered one of the Bible verses that was read out at the funeral; "Blessed are they that mourn: for they shall be comforted". – Matthew 5:4.

And that's exactly how it was. I was comforted. And though I was fine for a long time after that, nearly two years later I was beginning to question whether those two events really were a message from God, or just a coincidence. And it was beginning to play on my mind, and I felt the peace that God had given to me nearly two years earlier, was starting to erode. "O ye of little faith!"

Then, on the 1st of August 2011, I received an email from my dad about the helicopter that flew over the house on that rainy day. He was awake last night and started thinking about the helicopter that flew over the house. With the aid of a website, he worked out that it was flying in a 65-degree direction – the same direction that you would take if you were to fly direct between Alexandra in New Zealand where Dad's house was, and Pinckney in the United States where Tim was living at the time of his death! What are the odds of that? I was amazed again! Not only that God had hidden a message within a message, but that Dad would even think about the direction that the helicopter was flying in at all!

Like I said at the beginning of this section, God knows the hearts and minds of all people, and knows what they need, when they need it. God knew I needed this at this point, and saw fit to deliver it to me when I needed it.

Therefore, the peace that He had given to me nearly two years earlier was restored to me, right when I needed it, and I have never questioned the authenticity of the message behind it ever again. I have no need to. My peace was restored.

God proved that it was a legitimate message from Him to us, and it brought comfort to us when we needed it. God is good!

THIRD MESSAGE

Just before Christmas on Christmas Eve 2009, we received an email from our U.S.-based lawyer about Tim. Though she had never met Tim, she had a dream about him the night before. Here's what she said:

"P.S. I had a dream about Tim last night! (It seemed so real). I saw a helicopter coming towards my house and I saw Tim wave to me, I waved back and he landed the helicopter in the field next to my house. He turned the helicopter off and joined a picnic I was having with alot of people that I didn't recognize. He sat down and seemed to know everyone there, he asked me for a cup of coffee, but as I was bringing it out my alarm clock went off! The dream seemed very real and special. He looked real happy, handsome, slender, healthy and very self assured. Was Tim a coffee drinker? I remember offering him an assortment of cold drinks (it was a hot day) and thinking that it was strange that he was the only one at the party who wanted a hot coffee)! Anyway, that was my dream, who knows where all this comes from!"

Yes, Tim was a coffee drinker! But it went much further than that! He had taken a coffee class, his favourite website was a coffee website, and he was basically just an all-round coffee-buff! So this was a pretty amazing dream! More importantly however, was the timing of that dream. It seemed as if it was timed to get us through the Christmas season, when you think of loved ones more keenly than you do at other times.

To me, this was another message from God, designed to encourage us through the holiday period. It was the first Christmas since Tim had died, six months earlier.

FURTHER READING

For further reading, please see my website at
www.stevemoxham.com